Practical Know-how
in the Garden

SIMON &
SCHUSTER

LONDON • NEW YORK • SYDNEY • TORONTO

First published in Great Britain by
Simon & Schuster UK Ltd 2007
A CBS Company

ISBN 1 8473 7005 5
EAN 978 1 8473 7005 1

Simon and Schuster UK Ltd
Africa House
64–78 Kingsway
London WC2B 6AH

1 3 5 7 9 10 8 6 4 2

Design and illustrations by Jane Norman
Text by Jenny Kieldsen
Jacket design by Kari Brownlie
Printed and bound in China

Contents

Introduction

Whether you opt for flowers, vegetables or herbs, there are plenty of tips in this handy book on which varieties to choose and how to care for them. There are hints on recycling everyday household items – egg boxes, for example, make excellent seed trays, while used coffee grounds turn an alkaline soil more acid. If you don't have a garden but want to grow your own food, consider an allotment – there's sound advice on choosing one for your needs. Last but not least, make sure your garden is a welcome place for birds and other friendly wildlife, while keeping slugs and snails well away from your precious plants.

" *Our bodies are our gardens... our wills are our gardeners.* **"**

William Shakespeare, 1564–1616

General Garden Tips

To germinate peas, beans and sweet pea seeds

Soak the seeds in cold water for 24 hours. This is called 'chitting' and helps the tough outer shell of the seed to break open, which in turn speeds up germination.

Natural fertilizers

Crushed egg shells – work them into the soil well.

*

Used coffee grounds provide acid in alkaline soil.

*

Water from a fish tank or goldfish bowl is full of nutrients – use it on outdoor pot plants.

*

Water from boiled noodles or pasta: leave it to cool and use to water plants; they love the starch in the water.

❝ *The bad gardener quarrels with his rake* **❞**

American proverb

" Kind hearts are the gardens,
Kind thoughts are the roots,
Kind words are the flowers,
Kind deeds are the fruits,
Take care of your garden
And keep out the weeds,
Fill it with sunshine
Kind words and kind deeds "

Henry Wadsworth Longfellow, 1807–1882

Egg-box seed trays

Use cardboard egg boxes as seed trays.
Plant 2–3 seeds in each cup. When they come
through, pinch out the weaker ones and let the
strong one grow on. When ready to plant out,
cut the boxes into individual cups and put them
straight into the garden. The plant roots will
grow undisturbed and the cardboard will
gradually disintegrate.

Toilet-roll planters

The cardboard middles from toilet rolls can no longer be taken into school for children to use in crafts, so this is a new use for them. They are particularly good for growing peas, beans, and sweet peas. In winter, save the cardboard centres from toilet rolls. Stand them upright and fill with compost. Once the seeds have germinated in the seed tray, plant a single seedling in each toilet roll. The cardboard roll can be planted in soil and will slowly disintegrate.

To make plant labels

Cut the bottom out of a plastic yogurt pot and then cut the side of the pot into strips. Use a permanent marker pen to write on the strips of plastic, leaving room for pushing the ends into the soil. Hey presto!

To make ties for tall plants

This is useful for tomato plants and tall or large perennials. Old tights and stockings make great ties – they are strong and flexible yet soft enough not to cut into the plant stems.

66 *A Garden is a Friend You Can Visit Anytime* 99

Anon.

❝ *As for marigolds, poppies, hollyhocks, and valorous sunflowers, we shall never have a garden without them, both for their own sake, and for the sake of old-fashioned folks, who used to love them.* **❞**

Henry Ward Beecher, 1813–1887

To stake tall perennials

Always do this early. You can bet your life that if you think 'I must do that tomorrow', there will be high winds that night and your favourite plants will be blown to the ground. Use bamboo canes and string or try some of the new propriety products on offer in the garden centre. The other advantage of staking plants early is that they grow over or around the stakes to hide them effectively.

To fit a garden hose

To help push the hose on to a tap or into a
fitting try rubbing the inside of the hose with
some soap. This eases it on to the tap or fitting
and the soap will quickly dry afterwards.

To remove rust from garden tools

Use a stiff wire brush to remove the rust and
then scrape over the dull edges with a
metal file. Rub in some linseed oil.

To smooth wooden handles
on garden tools

This removes splinters and conditions the
wood. Rub rough handles with light sand paper
and then rub in some linseed oil. This will
protect the wood and stop it splitting
and cracking again.

To clean plastic patio furniture

Grimy plastic garden furniture will come clean
really quickly when you give it a good scrub with
a solution of washing soda. Allow ½ cup
soda to 600 ml (1 pt) water.

*" A healthy garden is a reflection of
a healthy soul."*

Anon.

Feeding the birds

If using bread, try brown or wholemeal. Whiz the crusts, a couple of the last slices and some peanuts in the food processor to make it easier for the birds to eat. In very cold weather, add a few porridge oats as well. It's best to put the mixture on a high bird table to discourage local cats from stalking the birds.

❝ *Two birds disputed about a kernel, when a third swooped down and carried it off* ❞

African proverb

" Criticizing another's garden doesn't keep the weeds out of your own "

Proverb

Dealing with Pests and Weeds

To make bird scarers

Unwanted CDs are fantastic for this. Thread
string through their middles and tie the CDs on
a stick or bamboo pole, where they will twist
in the wind and catch the light to deter birds.

Squirrel-proof bird feeders

To stop the squirrels getting all the peanuts you put out for the birds, look out for small feeders that fix on the window with plastic suction pads. These can be located in the middle of a window where there is nowhere for squirrels to grab on. The window-pane may get a little messy but the pleasure of seeing the birds close up makes it worthwhile.

"There is no gardening without humility.
Nature is constantly sending even its oldest
scholars to the bottom of the class for
some egregious blunder."

Alfred Austin, 1835–1910

To beat slugs and snails

Try sprinkling bran around your plants.
Slugs are attracted to it but it kills them. It also
attracts snails: they will assemble around it
making it easy to collect them.

Bury a plastic cup, up to the rim, in soil near
your plants and half fill it with beer or lager. The
slugs will drink the beer, fall in and drown.

Sprinkle gravel or crushed eggshells around
your favourite plants, which you know the snails
and slugs love. They do not like to crawl over
gravel – imagine how uncomfortable it must be!

To discourage moles

Human hair is an irritant to moles! If you cut your children's or family's hair: save it or ask the hairdresser for a bag of clippings. Remove the molehill and you will see the hole where the mole has pushed up the soil. Push some hair into this and, hopefully, the mole will move on. The soil from the molehill is fantastic with potting compost for potting and planting; you will find that it has become soft and aerated by the mole's digging.

To deter green fly on roses

Try planting garlic cloves around each rose
bush. This may not be 100 per cent effective,
but it does help and you do have the bonus
of harvesting freshly grown garlic.

" But he that dares not grasp the thorn
Should never crave the rose. "

Anne Bronte, 1820–1849

To get rid of weeds on paths and patios

This is useful for those weeds that grow through the cracks in your drive and patio. Add half a cup of salt to a gallon of cold water and stir until it dissolves. Water the weeds well with the salt solution.

To prevent weeds growing in cracks

Sprinkle dry salt directly into the actual crack or
hole; this also works well in the area around
the edge of your house.

"A good garden may have some weeds"

Thomas Fuller, 1608–1661

"How fair is a garden amid the trials and passions of existence."

Benjamin Disraeli, 1804–1881

The Vegetable Garden

Preparing your plot

If you have plenty of space – or an allotment –
divide your plot into 1.2-metre (4 foot) wide
growing beds. This is a good, manageable size.

" *Even the richest soil, if left uncultivated,*
will produce the rankest weeds. **"**

Leonardo da Vinci, 1452–1519

Rotating crops

Work out a planting rotation plan to keep crops moving around the plot, rather than planting the same type of vegetable in the same place year after year; this helps to prevent pests and diseases from taking hold.

66 *They're like two peas in a pod* 99

Proverb

Peas

Dig the soil well and dig in manure. In dry
weather they should be mulched and well
supported with sticks or stakes, allowing good
space for the pods to develop on the plants.

Broad beans

Dig the soil well and dig in manure. Plant the beans 15 cm (6 in) apart. Pick out the top shoots when the lower pods are set and you will get well-filled pods throughout the season.

" Weather means more when you have a garden. There's nothing like listening to a shower and thinking how it is soaking in around your green beans."

Marcelene Cox

French beans

Plant in a sunny position, protected from the wind, and give plenty of water. French beans also need to be picked regularly while they are young and tender.

Runner beans

They require deeply dug soil, lots of manure and huge amounts of water. Put your bean poles in early. Set them deep and secure them well – you will not believe how heavy the plants become when laden with beans. You can also grow runner beans on a tripod of bamboo canes set amongst flowers, or in a large tub.

Tomatoes

Grow tomatoes in your greenhouse, in a grow-bag or in the garden. Don't bother growing from seed (unless you're an expert), but buy small plants. Gardener's Delight is one of the best varieties to try the first time: these are tiny tomatoes, about the size of walnuts, very sweet and juicy, and they're not available in the shops. Nip out the growing tip at the top of the plant when you have five or six healthy looking trusses (fruit-bearing side shoots). Water and feed the plants well.

" It's difficult to think anything but pleasant thoughts while eating a home-grown tomato."

Lewis Grizzard, 1946–1994

To protect marrows and onions

During the summer months, while they are still growing, place a house tile or flat stone under marrows (and onion bulbs). This keeps it dry during the day and warm at night.

*"Life is an onion and one cries
while peeling it."*

French proverb

To store apples and pears

If you have fruit trees, pick the fruit when it's ripe. Check each fruit to ensure there is no bruising or insect infestation – it takes just one or two dodgy fruit to develop mould and spread this to the rest. Find a cool, airy, dark place to store them – a good secure shed that is not invaded by mice is ideal. Lay out the fruit on newspaper, not letting them touch each other. Ventilated cardboard boxes or cardboard cup holders (that you get in sandwich shops) are good for stacking or keeping apples. If you store it well, you should be able to continue eating the fruit until the following spring.

"*Judge a tree from its fruit,
not from its leaves***"**

Euripides, c. 480–406 BC

" In March and in April,
from morning to night,
In sowing and setting good
housewives delight;
To have in a garden, or other like plot
To trim up their houses,
and furnish their pot."

Thomas Tusser, 1524–1580

Allotments

How to get an allotment

Contact your local council to find out what they can offer and whether there is a waiting list. Leases are usually for a year and costs are very reasonable (perhaps as little as £10 a year).

Check the rules

Ask if you are allowed to keep chickens, or rabbits or bees. Find out if you are allowed to plant fruit trees. Are you allowed to sell produce, for example, at a communal village stall? What are the rules about sheds? You may wish to know if there are reduced rates for pensioners.

Allotments

" *Plant your seeds in a row,*
One for the pheasant, one for the crow,
One to rot and one to grow. "

Garden lore

Visit the allotment first

Visit on a Sunday afternoon when everyone will be toiling away and it is a good opportunity to find out all sorts of important information.

Is the ground ever waterlogged?

✻

Are some plots better than others?

✻

Is there any problem with vandalism?

✻

Is there good access to water?

✻

Do you pay extra for water, and do hosepipe bans apply?

Is there an allotment society and do you pay towards it?

Do they try to encourage mostly organic gardening?

Do they hold an annual show?

" *As is the gardener, so is the garden* **"**

Proverb

Children friendly

If you're going to take your young children, make sure there is a safe place to play or give them their own plot to dig.

What to grow?

Most allotment holders grow vegetables and fruit, but if you have a large plot, it can look beautiful at certain times of year with colourful blooms such as sunflowers or marigolds or even a wild flower patch.

How to prepare

You may find that your plot hasn't been touched for years and is a tangle of weeds, in which case clear it bit by bit. The best time to start doing this is autumn or early winter. Ask if anyone has a Rotavator you can borrow to dig up your plot for sowing.

"Keep love in your heart. A life without it is like a sunless garden when the flowers are dead."

Oscar Wilde, 1854–1900

The Flower Garden

Quick climber

Clematis montana grows quickly and blooms in the spring; other species of clematis, though they have exotic flowers, can be more difficult to grow.

Sweet-smelling flowers

These are a special treat to grow and are often fragrant in the early evening, which makes sitting outside with a drink a great pleasure for the senses.

Annuals: night-scented stocks, tobacco plants (Nicotiana) and sweet peas

Biannuals: Bromptom stocks and some scented pinks; don't forget Lily of the valley

Climbing plants: honeysuckle – be sure to buy a sweet smelling variety as some are not highly perfumed. *Jasmine officinale* is an amazingly fragrant plant.

" Here are sweet-peas, on tip-toe for a flight:
With wings of gentle flush o'er delicate white,
And taper fingers catching at all things,
To bind them all about with tiny rings."

John Keats, 1795–1821

Success with roses

It is often said that it is a good idea to buy roses from a supplier north of where you live as this gives them a good chance of growing well in your (more southerly) area.

" *And I wove the thing to a random rhyme,*

For the Rose is Beauty, the Gardener,

Time. **"**

Austin Dobson, 1840–1921

✳

" *Be both the gardener and the rose.* **"**

Anon.

" *Earth laughs in flowers.* **"**

Ralph Waldo Emerson, 1803–1882

Wild flowers

Leave a corner of your garden for wild flowers. Grow from packets, or plants that can sometimes be bought at garden centres, or simply let wild flowers 'arrive'. If any other unorthodox plant or grass seeds itself elsewhere in the garden, transplant it to your wild area. Remember not to add any fertilizers to your wild garden.

" In the spring time, the only pretty ring time,

When birds do sing, hey ding a ding;

Sweet lovers love the spring. "

William Shakespeare, 1564–1616

Early spring bulbs

As you will probably not be spending much time outside in the garden in early spring, try and plant spring bulbs where you will see them from the house. Snowdrops and other small bulbs will be the first flowers of the year.

To dead-head spring bulbs

As soon as the flowers fade, remove them with secateurs. This ensures that the bulbs put their energy into next year's flowers. Leave the leaves as they are – they will gradually turn yellow and can be cut back after six weeks. Don't tie the leaves into neat bundles.

❝_May flowers always line your path and sunshine light your day. May songbirds serenade you every step along the way. May a rainbow run beside you in a sky that's always blue. And may happiness fill your heart each day your whole life through._**❞**

Irish Blessing

"I've made an odd discovery. Every time I talk to a savant I feel quite sure that happiness is no longer a possibility. Yet when I talk with my gardener, I'm convinced of the opposite."

Bertrand Russell, 1872–1970

Russian vine

This is great if you need to cover something ugly – like a fence or a shed – quickly! However, it is so fast growing that it could spread all over your garden and take over...so take care.

To transplant house-potted hyacinths

After flowering indoors, put hyacinths and other small bulbs, such as crocuses, outside to die down naturally. Plant the bulbs in the garden where they will flower next year and for many years afterwards. This works for bulbs you planted yourself and for bought flowering bulbs.

> *"Faith sees a beautiful blossom in a bulb,*
> *a lovely garden in a seed, and a*
> *giant oak in an acorn."*

William Arthur Ward, 1921–1994

To dead-head flowers

If you have the patience and time to cut off
flowers that are past their best, you'll see your
plants continue to bloom. Do this at least every
other day. Cut off rose heads as though you are
pruning, and perennials down to the ground;
just take the heads off annuals.

> **"** *Flowers are restful to look at. They have neither emotions nor conflicts.* **"**

Sigmund Freud, 1856–1939

> **"** *It matters not what goal you seek – Its secret here reposes: You've got to dig from week to week – To get Results or Roses.* **"**

Edgar Guest, 1862–1959

" *A man's nature runs either to herbs, or to weeds; therefore let him seasonably water the one, and destroy the other.* **"**

Sir Francis Bacon, 1561–1626

The Herb Garden

Planting the herb garden

Think of the times when it's wet, cold, or both,
and plant herbs as near to your kitchen
door as possible.

Starting your herbs

Don't buy herbs for the garden from the
supermarket as these are primarily bred to
grow on your window-sill for little more than a
week. If you're an expert, try growing herbs
from seed; if not, just buy plants. Most herbs
prefer sunny, well-drained soil and
very little feeding.

Chives

They are easy to grow and should be watered
during dry spells as their small bulbous roots
are close to the surface. Cut the flower heads
off regularly (small purple pompoms), otherwise
they will run to seed and the stalks will become
tough. They live for a long time and enjoy a
good feed; otherwise their tips go yellow.
Cutting can continue until the first frosts,
when they will die back and reappear
in early spring.

"*Everything on the earth has a purpose,
every disease an herb to cure it,
and every person a mission.***"**

Anon.

Marjoram (oregano)

There are many types so be sure to buy a plant that is a perennial. The summer flowers are a great attraction for bees. Plant in a sunny place and trim back well in the autumn.

Mint

Best planted in containers as the prolific
varieties can take over your garden in no time.
If you bury the pots the roots are capable of
breaking through and romping away!

*❝ Grow mint in the garden to attract
money to your purse. ❞*

Folklore

Bay

Plant a small bay tree in a tub in good soil and place it in a sunny spot. Protect it in frosty weather. If you're lucky enough to have an established bay tree, it responds to a good pruning in the spring.

Sage

There are over 500 different types of sage and many are flowering garden plants. *Officinalis* is the best variety for cooking. It will grow in most soils but prefers clay with good drainage and a sunny position. Cut it back to encourage growth and harvest the sprigs before the flowers appear.

❝ *Sage 'for teeming women, to helpe them the better forward in their childbearing.'* **❞**

John Parkinson, herbalist, 1567–1650

Thyme

Thyme is suitable for rock gardens and for growing between paving stones. Brushing past and bruising the leaves releases their fragrance. Lemon thyme is popular with bees. Cutting back will encourage growth. In a cold winter, protect plants with a little straw.

" *The opening summer, the sky,*

The shining moorland – to hear

The drowsy bee, as of old,

Hum o'er the thyme. **"**

Matthew Arnold, 1822–1888

Rosemary

Rosemary is difficult to get going, but once
established will flourish for years. Buy a biggish
plant, plant it in a sunny position and protect it
from frost in the first winter. Large flowering
spears look good in flower arrangements
and on a summer cheese board.

" The distilled water of rosemary, drunk morning and evening, 'taketh away the stench of the mouth and the breath.'"

John Gerard, herbalist, 1545–1612

Parsley

Parsley is a biennial that can be tricky to grow.
It likes some shade and a soil rich in humus.
Keep it well watered in dry weather and keep
harvesting the leaves and cutting back the
stalks; otherwise the plants will flower
and go to seed.

" It takes an honest man to grow Parsley well. "

" Parsley only grows where the missus is master. "

Garden lore

Basil

An annual herb, basil cannot withstand frost
but is easily grown from seed. Plant the seeds
in early spring (indoors or in the greenhouse)
and prick out into individual pots that you can
keep either in the greenhouse or on a sunny
window-sill. The leaves can burn in direct sun.
Be sure to keep picking the leaves and nip out
the top shoots to encourage bushy growth
and prevent the plant from flowering.

" *With Basil then I will begin*
Whose scent is wondrous pleasing. **"**

Michael Drayton, 1563–1631

Preserving basil

Make pesto – an Italian paste of basil with pine nuts, garlic, Parmesan cheese and olive oil – and freeze the paste. Alternatively, whiz basil and olive oil in a liquidizer and freeze initially in an ice cube tray to make handy-sized cubes for flavouring sauces.

Tarragon

French tarragon is the only tarragon plant worth
growing. It is not an annual but is delicate and
best treated as such. It likes well-drained soil
that is not heavy – and definitely no frost. It can
be grown indoors but you don't need to water
it more than once or twice a week.

" During the Middle Ages, tarragon was sometimes worn in the shoes of those on pilgrimage. "

Garden lore

Drying herbs

Thyme, bay leaves, rosemary and sage are the best herbs to dry. Cut the stems as long as you can and tie into loose bunches. Hang upside down in a warm dark place – an airing cupboard is perfect. When the leaves are brittle enough to crumble, remove the leaves and store in airtight jars in a cool dark place for no more than a year.

How deeply seated in the human heart is the liking for gardens and gardening.

Alexander Smith, 1830–1867

" Gardens are a form of autobiography. "

Sydney Eddison, garden writer